TWISTED SHAPES OF LIGHT

The Poiema Poetry Series

Poems are windows into worlds; windows into beauty, goodness, and truth; windows into understandings that won't twist themselves into tidy dogmatic statements; windows into experiences. We can do more than merely peer into such windows; with a little effort we can fling open the casements, and leap over the sills into the heart of these worlds. We are also led into familiar places of hurt, confusion, and disappointment, but we arrive in the poet's company. Poetry is a partnership between poet and reader, seeking together to gain something of value—to get at something important.

Ephesians 2:10 says, "We are God's workmanship . . ." *poiema* in Greek—the thing that has been made, the masterpiece, the poem. The Poiema Poetry Series presents the work of gifted poets who take Christian faith seriously, and demonstrate in whose image we have been made through their creativity and craftsmanship.

These poets are recent participants in the ancient tradition of David, Asaph, Isaiah, and John the Revelator. The thread can be followed through the centuries—through the diverse poetic visions of Dante, Bernard of Clairvaux, Donne, Herbert, Milton, Hopkins, Eliot, R. S. Thomas, and Denise Levertov—down to the poet whose work is in your hand. With the selection of this volume you are entering this enduring tradition, and as a reader contributing to it.

—D. S. Martin
Series Editor

Twisted Shapes of Light

WILLIAM JOLLIFF

CASCADE *Books* · Eugene, Oregon

TWISTED SHAPES OF LIGHT

Cascade Books
An Imprint of Wipf and Stock Publishers
199 W. 8th Ave., Suite 3
Eugene, OR 97401

www.wipfandstock.com

ISBN 13: 978-1-4982-0840-6

Cataloging-in-Publication data:

William Jolliff.

    Twisted shapes of light / William Jolliff.

    p.; 23 cm—Includes bibliographical references and index.

    ISBN 13: 978-1-4982-0840-6

    1. 2. 3. 4. I. II.

CALL NUMBER 2015

Manufactured in the USA.

For Jacob Henry, Rebecca Peace, and Anna Fulton

That was the true Light, which lighteth every man and woman that cometh into the world. He was in the world, and the world was made by him, and the world knew him not.

Table of Contents

Table of Contents

Part One

Age and Belief

Age and Belief

Once age begins to draw its tether, every wisp
of faith is like a breath beneath the surface of the sea.

God exists? Maybe. God knows? Possibly.
God's concerned? Debatable. So the snare pulls

tight around the tan slim bodies we used
to count on. At first we seriously think

about chewing off a leg, but opt today
for pleated pants and shoes that don't make

our feet feel like strung hams, and we pay
extra for lenses just thinner than ice cubes,

forgetting the time when lips formed easy *ahs*
and spoke to God as if he were a drugstore clerk

somewhere in the center of Kansas, who asks
Can I help you find anything? You just holler

if you need me, anything at all, and sometimes
we did call, and believed that he, and we, heard.

Forgiveness released us with the ease of a whisper,
peace rained each morning like flakes of yeasty manna,

and *I believe* was as easy to say as *yes yes yes*.

Ways to Die

When you think of all the ways to kill a man,
as I sometimes do,
you see pretty soon that some ways
take you away from your fellows and kin
while others throw you in, all in.

There's the twisted pharmaceutical weirdness
of chemical injection—
something as lovely as the rest before sleep
puts a dark cloak over its hollow-eyed head
and the next thing you know, some poor boy's dead.

And once I saw a film-maker's version of *the chair,*
in Texas I suppose,
and you know right away why they use the hood—
you could see the body, not quite human,
wrench its twisting self into a pained oblivion.

I'm not quite sure why Romans used crucifixion
to murder our Lord,
but if the pictures and the pendants tell the truth,
He died with His spirit already on the rise,
His arms spread as wide as the look in His eyes.

Pictures of Katie

I never said it was possible, I only said it was true.
—Sir William Crookes, 1832–1919

Say your brother died of some disease.
It could've been anyone, anything,
but the brother was Philip, and you were close,
and the disease was yellow fever.
What would you do?

Become yourself in time,
president of the *Chemical Society*,
the *Association for the Advancement of Science*,
even the *Royal Academy*—

the circle that, forty years before,
had shunned those desperate studies
closest to your heart, even after you'd given
them thallium, tagged and weighed.

You surely loved your poisons, especially that:
so blue, so soft it leaves its mark on paper,
but a signature so pale you can't be sure,
always sure, you see it.

And you would invent the radiometer,
the Crookes tube, the spinthariscope,
discover cathode rays, and even be knighted—
but not until you'd spoken with Philip

once, then sought him again through every
channel in England—even Florence Cook—
and discovered that the medium is almost,
but not always, the message.

And you wouldn't have believed Miss Cook
had the proof not been your own cameras,
your laboratory, your 44 pictures
of pretty Katie King,

the most desirable of spirit guides.
What did Philip think?
You died a knight at 86.
Some brothers live longer than others,
but we all spend good years chasing the dead.

Small College, Small Town

Family genius? Your last term with me, you slumped
in the back row with the damned-if-I-care crowd,
your serious hair a coal black curtain between us.

Has it been a dozen years? I've watched you
push your strollers down the cracked off-campus walks,
watched you walk your kids to school, watched them

walk you to school, then run ahead, then go alone.
Now I remember why I remember. It matters to me
when students don't engage—the classroom's my stage,

and I want you all to love the show. Your presence
was spotty; your work regular, if not quite good.
But when I click the years it all makes sense:

You were sick. Your last semester was your first
trimester. I'm sorry. You were listening to me
babble through *The Scarlet Letter,* wondering if

you were going to pitch your breakfast. Then
halfway through exam week, you were married,
the right thing to do in this little town, to a boy

who aced my first-year comp, but never spoke.
I hope he's treating you better now—he was nice
enough, but strangely quiet even then. It's odd

you bought that house on the edge of campus.
For years I've given you my *Winesburg* nod
as an old and kindly former prof should, but

you've always dodged it, there, behind that veil
of hair. So maybe you're still trying to find
the back row of town. Or trying to lose your *A.*

Diet of Worms

Holiness is a discipline. It demands attention.
To begin, play games, but quit before winning.

Touch a soft brown arm, but never, never kiss.
Play heaven's music, but never end a song.

It's like any other diet. Protein supplements
will keep you alive, and you will learn, someday,

to feel full. What must be beaten daily is
that misbegotten longing for something sweet.

Sunday Vigil on the Corner

Four years into this war, a handful of us stand,
herringbone-respectable, gray, well-trimmed,
sober as bankers in mackinaws and new boots,

not a shred of tie-dye in sight, our neat signs
square as cartoon trees against the continual
Oregon drizzle. It's our First-Sunday Ritual.

We try to mingle, abandoned to ourselves in public
discomfort, stranded by hard old belief, right here
at Second and Adams. Our fingers freeze with reason:

"Invest in Peace," "Children Matter," "Peace is Patriotic."
We straighten red silk ties and rub clean chins,
chapped against the wind. The cold keeps soaking in.

Passersby honk Volvos. Some smile, some shake
their heads, puzzled. Some flash our ancient holy sign,
others flick us the finger. We wrap our scarves

tighter. At last a rusty beater rumbles by, packed
with acned teens, shouting as we knew they would:
"Go back to Russia, you f*****g hippies."

And we laugh. Finally someone's found us out,
stared straight through what time and tweed cannot
disguise. A car on fire with those most likely to die—

few prospects, no money, sure of nothing but
their own anger. We look around our aging crowd,
remembering some of the ways a heart can break.

Lunch with the Lord's Anarchists

At the Jesus Radicals Conference

They walk through the line in an orderly way,
taking enough, but not too much. No one laughs.
They bring their own plates and cups. No Styrofoam.

Potluck veteran though I am, I can't make out the food,
but I'm sure it's deeply committed and fairly traded.
It's strange to hear such passionate talk in a church.

We move to the lawn of the Mennonites who agreed
to host the gathering. More accustomed to capitalistic
market-driven hygiene, I'm glad we've come outside.

Because I ask, some tell me outlines of their journeys,
of where they came from, how they wound up here.
There are many wrinkled ways to get to Portland.

Finished, they slump in quiet piles of natural fiber,
and at last I can read their bodies. Truths dangle
from pierced flesh and cover every inch of visible skin.

Jesus, I am old and academic, and I have much to learn.
I would like to read the rest of them, the rest of their stories.

Ramblin' Seth Plays the Red & Black Cafe

And when the day of Pentecost was fully come,
they were all with one accord in one place. (Acts 2:1)

Maybe they gathered in a room just like this,
a coffee shop somewhere in Jerusalem,
not on the outskirts exactly, but just
on the seedier edge of downtown.

Maybe some sweetly pierced Martha-like
hipster was pulling fresh shots in the back,
and her sister, Our Mary of the Many Tattoos,
was already slipping the day-old scones

to the masses, those unwashed and quizzical
lovers of God who just heard the good word
that Seth had come home to this place, safe
and dry, and warmer than the sidewalk.

Some sit on tipped-back chairs, a handful rest
quasi-lotus on the floor, drumming their thighs,
growing content in their own woven grunge
(the affect turned real as the money ran out).

Then Seth takes the stage, lighting his candles,
tuning a little, then lighting some more,
the hemp and soy and *happy-birthday* candles,
dollar-store votives for remaindered saints.

He tries for mellow, but mellow won't come
or won't last past the first two tunes, no matter
how soft his *Hello, everyone.* If passion is
a simmering kettle of stew, his will scorch.

Before the first chorus it's already burning:
each song is a message in tongues. And then
one little stick of scented oil glows brighter.
It rises, floats, and settles on his dreads.

The big bare feet begin to stomp, and there comes
from heaven a sound like a rushing wind,
and they are bewildered, because they all
hear him speak their own language.

The Labyrinth Speaks

I knew they would come from the very pour.
I could just as easily have been the floor
of someone's garage, a bicycle rack,

a boat ramp, a barn, a sidewalk, sure to crack—
so this path seemed my destiny
charted in the stars before I came to be.

In the circling strokes of the stainer's brush
I knew each pilgrim's sole, each holy touch,
and felt each weight, the tapping of each stick,

the pacing desperation of the sick,
the sorrow of lovers, their bitterness,
each shivering touch, each unreturned caress,

the leaden chest that heaves when faith is lost,
the hollowness of unbelief, the cost
that must be paid for quiet vanities,

the rage that robs the over-wise of peace.
Some come to beg forgiveness, some to rant.
Some come to pray; some come because they can't.

I serve them all, and on my concrete way
they learn as much as their steps will let me say.
Like any winter road, I've felt the burn of salt,

the throb of loss, when the heart's like a vault
without a key. But sometimes doors fall open.
I'm only the stone, but I help that happen.

Big Bang

Just when I'm tempted to believe
that my fundamentalist neighbors
have taken the admonition to heart—
Hope is dangerous, kill it young—

I hike by their church-school at noon
and hear the holy thunder: children
file silently through the fire doors, then
explode like a storm of Bazooka bubbles,

blue plaid jumpers and creased khakis
scattering and rolling like billiard balls
across the felt-green, tightly-cropped park
of a playground, jet-propelled by shouts

that echo with a morning's elation,
cries as bright and lusty as those of their
publicly-educated peers, maybe more.
The air is electric with the freshest

of flesh, swinging and hanging, even
dancing from the bars of parti-colored,
evangelically-maintained jungle gyms,
while rippling clouds of sweaty freedom

rise over the undulating mass
of limbs, until at two bells they fall
back to the quiet brick, exhausted
but not quite dim, new creations,

the fire of damp cheeks and matted hair
bearing testimony that the lamp
within cannot be wholly dimmed,
even by bushels of the darkest belief.

The Elders Visit

And such a joy they are to see. Their shirts
alone are worth my time, such blinding white
against their creased black slacks, sensible shoes,
and shining paperbacks: keys for my salvation.

Come in, fellows! I ask about their mission,
their months away from family and home,
and how the Lord is blessing them in Oregon.
And I ask them to tell me about God. They do.

But sir, have you read the Book of Mormon?. . .
Hmm. So this Smith, was he quite the scholar
of old Semitic languages? *No, not at all*!
Here their smiles bloom, their eyes turn to pearl:

No, they say, *just a third grade education.* . . .
The elders are sure I'll share their wonder.
And so I do, recalling deadly afternoons
in Dr. Reader's dungeon, each minute an hour,

each semester at least a millennium,
offering up my tortured mistranslations
of Plato, Sophocles, worn pieces of Xenophon,
sweating each particle and grave accent,

assured that no amount of angsty sweat
would ever fix them. Then years of Paul,
growing still more sinful with my syntax,
finding God's grace in the order of words.

Then risking my soul over backwards Hebrew,
cracking badly one Sunday afternoon,
kicking the lexicon around my rented room,
breaking its spine as it had broken mine.

The elders are kind, their pious faces bright.
He was inspired, they say, *he was Spirit-led.*
Jesus, such perfect sweetness on their lips.
I nearly wish it could be true—not the tales,

not the *mythoi* of Lehi and Joseph Smith,
but the miracle of such translation.
I tell the young elders I'm glad they've come.
I tell them should they ever start to doubt

the book, their souls will never lose their home
in the love of the Lord, and this old Friend
will always be good for a supper or two.
And I hope they know I mean it. I do.

A Blessing: Eleanor, Lila, Ellen and Mack

The Lord lift up His countenance upon thee and give thee peace.
(Numbers 6:26)

When Eleanor hears "How Great Thou Art,"
her hands, suddenly cups, lift their offerings.
Once raised, they wave her through each hymn
she loved before her stroke. She knows the words.

Lila—that's Spanish, she says, *Lee-lah*—
is a veritable technical manual
at least here, a fine mind whose body
just gave way. Singing keeps her heart in time.

Ellen's eyes grow moist with each new joy:
ham cubes, cooked carrots, and "Amazing Grace"—
it's all so good. Her chair alarm keeps quiet
the whole hour. She licks her lips with music.

Mackey's bent jaw drifts hard to starboard,
but "What a Friend We Have in Jesus"
brings him about. After that, he takes my hands.
His face shines. *I'm Maa. . . Maa. . . Maa. . . Hill.*

Eleanor, Lila, Ellen, and Mackey
are glad we've come. It was a good day.
Ellen rolls back to bed, but the others stay
up to watch cars go by. When we leave

they wave our benediction through the glass.

Part Two

Reach Hither Thy Finger

The Price of Salvation

Sometimes even good students tell me lies,
usually about something small: fine old books
they haven't really read, their test scores,

occasionally weekend escapades.
I'm pretty sure they notice I can tell
or suspect it at least, and sometimes

I can. But I don't mind. What troubles me
is why, when they do, their faces fade
into a foggy light, and I see instead

the face of a traveling preacher, Peter Swartz,
the man who *led me to the Lord* at eight,
kneeling by the altar at Culver Creek Church,

chanting the power of the Holy Word of God
even while his forehead took on an oily glow
and his eyes drifted separately toward heaven

or maybe just drifted away. Who cares?
He was just an old ex-pastor put out to stud,
a week here, a week there. And I'm sure

he wanted his words to be real as much as anyone—
his story, all the stories, fine and old and true.

The Wise and Foolish Virgins Redux

And the foolish said unto the wise, "Give us of your oil, for our lamps are gone out." But the wise answered, saying, "Not so; lest there be not enough for us and you. . . ." (Matthew 25: 8–9)

Lord, that parable raises certain doubts.
Since most English majors are women,
I've spent the better part of my career
teaching a room full of virgins, almost.

Overall, the women in my classes
pay attention, ask unguarded questions,
speak with admirable compassion,
worry about their grades, and smile.

But remember to purchase a sufficient
quantity of any known commodity
to supply some wholly unforeseen
contingency? Five of ten? Jesus,

in twenty-five years of teaching,
maybe four. And of these, three
would have shared their last drops
with anyone (in the spirit of sisterhood).

True, the fourth, Laurel, would not
have shared half a bologna sandwich
with a starving kitten, lest the kitten
become too dependent. She became

a suburban pastor. But the others. . . .
Is *that* what the Kingdom of Heaven is like?
A world packed full of *Laurels*, without
the *Joannas*, *Cassandras*, and *Emilys*,

forgetting their pens, asking strange
questions, offering their last tissues
to any poor sister who overslept,
showed up late, and failed the test?

Touching Abishag

Let there be sought for my Lord the king a young virgin: and let her stand
before the king, and let her cherish him, and let her lie in thy bosom that my
lord the king may get heat. (I Kings 1:2)

Roused by the touch of her thigh in the night,
the old king reached a hand toward what he thought
was light, and found instead the weight of wool

against his hand, the tender shackle of his age.
He rolled back his eyes to what had been a dream,
and found only shadows where images had been

of shields, spears, and women, of songs sung in his name,
and he knew that while the flavor of desire may change,
he would never know desire's lack. The room was black,

save for an olive lamp the servants let the girl burn,
but he could see her cheek, feel her hips, her curving
waist beneath his feet, her dark hair soft against his heel.

Adam Walks

I heard thy voice in the garden, and I was afraid, because I was naked. . . .
(Genesis 3:10)

The morning after longing stopped,
Adam crossed through the garden, draped
his loins and face, and believed that all
the leaves had veiled would stay so.

What faith. Though he'd eaten from the tree,
he was, like its trunk, thorny and dumb.
So when in the cool of the day it called
his name, that same old voice,

he was only *half* afraid to be seen,
half afraid that his body would rise
up singing and wave a red confession.
His heart already stank of grace.

Later, when lust would rear its blood-mule
head, like a one-eyed child grinning, stumped
by a hard, fleshy puzzle, he'd contrive
to cut it off . . . for purity's sake. . . .

Yes. For the sake of the woman, he would
pare his fallen body like an apple,
as you might prune a withering vine.
But at dawn there came a voice, a hum,

a whistle, a tone like hers but less clear.
Echoes led what stump of brain he had away,
away to hard gray work, to the dead voices
of his children. And now Adam walks,

clothed in skins of beasts by wooden gods.
His arms reach out, and his fingers hook
through the sockets of Death's dark skull.
But the voice will not stop calling.

Elisha and the Limits of Grace

There came forth little children out of the city, and mocked him, and said unto him, "Go up, thou bald head; go up, thou bald head. . . ." (II Kings 2:23)

Our shiny-domed Sunday school teacher,
twice-born and wholly sanctified,
relished the tale of Elisha's she-bears.

After all, he was a prophet of God,
and those boys, all forty-two of them,
must have been sinful or worse

to heckle the Lord's own preacher
for being fat, maybe, like our teacher,
and bald, ditto. For little fundamentalists

that answer was a cup of cool water.
It spared us lots of worry, since we knew
one thing for sure: *we* would never do

what *they* did. We could *imagine* what
they'd done, and did, but that was *all*.
That was plenty. Even now, I wonder

if it pays to fill the twisted story in:
the forty-two mothers and forty-two
fathers and forty-two acts of love,

all brought to deadly naught by a pair
of divinely directed beasts
and God's overly sensitive prophet.

Such questions necessarily arise
whenever we try to believe in grace
or bank off its angles, so bloody and transient.

Noah's Children

All in whose nostrils was the breath of life, of all that was in the dry land, died. (Genesis 7:22)

For weeks, bloated bodies floated. Jetsam,
pale as candy-sticks, thumped against the hull.
But Noah's children learned not to hear,
even to forget

the frantic tap-thud-tap of birds trapped
in a leather bucket, then of fists and sticks
against the ark's thick sides. The water
rose slowly.

So everyone knew: the lunatic with elephant skin
was right. Without a shore, the living watched
the velvet sky, fancied devils in the stars.
They'd nowhere to go,

and the lights reminded them sometimes of cities,
of home, sometimes of torches: their drowning friends
had tried to fire the pitch-sealed doors, but began
too late. Fools.

And Noah's children have been lucky ever since,
have slept in the bellies of their arks whenever
weather threatens, or when their neighbors
lose their sense.

They watch, from rainbow windows, the stained light
of small fires.

Legion's Farewell to the Gerasenes

And the unclean spirits went out, and entered into the swine: and the herd ran violently down a steep place into the sea. (Mark 5:13)

You have to admit, I had my season.
Even among demons there's hierarchy—
hell, we invented it. Those devils down
on the low end, maybe they just rot fruit.
And some get their rocks off all morning
knocking cups of Starbucks onto laptops.
Others—we call them middle management—
like to specialize in nails and screws,
spread them in the *Visitors* lots at prisons.
Small stuff. Everyday grief enhancement.
Our old boys, once they start to get soft,
will settle in a spooky house, whoosh around
when some poor schizo creaks a floorboard,
and try to get themselves featured on local TV.

Not every bugger can possess a human.
It takes years of persistence, a thousand
vicious little acts, to earn yourself a soul:
constant nettling, secret petty vandalisms,
morphing words from how they were meant
to what they might be taken to mean.
Decades of digging ditches in the name
of, you guessed it, The Truth. And this:
pulling hearts back inside chests when
it would've been as easy to let them love.
So what if I was eventually re-assigned
to a herd of swine. Could you have done better?
Judge me by the quality of my competition.
Face it, chums: I had a helluva run.

Ananias's Confession

And the young men arose, wound him up, and carried him out, and buried him. (Acts 5:6)

It was evening, ebony dark, and I was full
of praise. Then the deal was cut, we drank,
and I remembered how hungry I had been,

how my belly had churned like a bag of snakes
just days before, before the Light and change
struck me with new friends, a new Word—new sight.

Since the wife and I didn't need a field, or anything
else, now, in the warmth of this new Body,
I let it go. And after all, Barnabas. . . .

How they'd praised the ones who sold and gave all,
and how we longed to feel such human comfort.
So we decided just to say, "Here it is, the money,"

which wasn't a lie, exactly. That she, my lover
who could be so hot and cold and who had
been with so many, would lose her nerve *then*—

who'd believe it? But I think I'm still forgiven.
I dropped as dead as sin, a regular Christ
ending that way, looking as I'd learned to,

for something to pay, something more to spend.

Reach Hither Thy Finger

"... thrust it into my side: and be not faithless, but believing." (John 20:27)

Maybe the wound still oozed, or maybe
it had healed over with scars like golden coins.
Thomas might have noticed, but I doubt it.

True, he placed his finger in the Lord's hand,
and his hand in the Lord's side,
and then, we presume, he held his heart

in the bleeding heart. I like to think that.
And I like to think that years later he was still
radiant with holy light. My unholy hunch, though,

is that within a week he learned to doubt
his eyes or his touch, maybe both, maybe
whether he'd really been in the room or not,

or if again the elders had sent him out
for bread or fish, anything to keep his mouth
out of earshot. He wasn't the type to suffer

his loss in silence, and the more he wondered,
the more they doubted, too. That's my guess.
And that may be why only John, the youngest

of the bunch, the mystic, the Lord's beloved,
recalled the very day, and cared enough
about belief to recall the shame of doubt.

Feeding the 5000, or How the Gospel Came To Oregon

When Jesus therefore perceived that they would come and take him by force,
to make him a king, he departed again into a mountain himself alone.
(John 6:15)

Five thousand hungry friends—what do you do?
Well, you feed them. Use whatever's at hand.
You take that kid's fish and barley loaves
and do what a savior does best, break them,

your body, give it away, let them have it all.
You knew what would happen, that it would
go south quick, but they were hungry and love
was always your bottom line. It's no wonder

they wanted to make you king. So to avoid
success at all costs, you did what others would do:
you ducked out and found your way to Oregon.
Maybe you did it in some magical god-way,

maybe you sailed the cape and up the coast,
maybe you caught a wagon train in St. Louis.
Any way you look at it, those good folks
in Palestine were fed, and Oregon found

a god—maybe the only kind of god that most
folks here could ever believe in: a quiet god
who would rather pitch a tent along the coast
than be king, who'd leave his borrowed camel

at the trailhead, grab a plastic bag of jerky,
a handful of raisins, maybe a fiddle, and go.
Nothing left to do now but boil a little coffee
and try like the devil to figure what comes next.

The Prophet Amos Adds a Postscript

Hear this word, ye kine of Bashan,
that are in the mountain of Samaria,
which oppress the poor, which crush the needy. . . . (Amos 4:1)

As I said, the Lord called me, took me away
from my flocks, told me, "Boy, give'm hell."
And it was nothing short of hell I gave them.
He showed me a vision, told me what to say.
So I left the farm, preached the Word, and
came back home. But I'm no lily of the field.

I've been around the rich too long to think
they'll give anything away. You don't corner
the market on oil and corn by being a fool.
Those mansions didn't grow there. When rich
babies are sucking a slave's teat, one thing
they learn is how to hold on. They'll hold on.

I'm a prophet, right? I know how sermons end:
The Lord will restore your cities and land,
the mountains shall drip with sweet wine. . . .
And all that. But I'm a farmer, too. I've been
scorched and flooded enough times to know
you can't get too darn sure about the weather.

Part Three

The Fleshy Ear of God

The Last Pasture

With faith in what the Lord might make,
they cut away the words of trees
and made the valleys whistle *farm:*
an old song, but one the natives here

had never sung. Some land got lost
along the way, some farmers lost their
lives, and, if we believe the stones,
most lost a child, many two.

That's the story of *here*, this place,
these acres a man with my name
deeded over to the township dead
for as long as the creeks shall flow.

I don't want it back. It's one field
rightly used. The other sacred ground
for miles around whispers *corn*
and *wheat* and *beans*, and its voice

is deep and green, but not quite true.
Something's missing from the soil.
The winds turn brown with change.
The farmers' children cough and spit.

Tonight we listen to what the world
might say, but the words don't fit
this tune, and what's been set apart,
Old John's churchyard, may be close

to all that we have left of holiness.

Steers in Winter

Christmas day we played the savior.
Overnight ice swallowed anything
close to green, and then the north wind
set in to freeze. From the high barn window,

we saw the cattle in the bottom ground
standing church-pew still, dumb, fat,
stupid, but mostly stunned with what
must've seemed the horror of Revelation.

We loaded bales on a flatbed wagon,
shot a John Deere's nose full of ether,
and skidded down the lane to the pasture gate.
With language and a hatchet, we thawed the chain.

But those Angus steers stood quiet as the damned.
Even when we slit the sisal twine
and kicked out sheaves, they stood like stones,
too cold to believe in the glorious grace of hay.

The Hardness of the Pews

I didn't mind the hardness of the pews then
and wouldn't now. If you've been perched
on a tractor seat since dawn—or, worse yet,
if you've hopped off it half a hundred times
to change a shear bolt or clear a jam of stalks,
Good Lord, a walnut board with some curve
that's shaped a little like a back is hardly short
of heaven. Or if you've been stacking hay,
packing back bales, the hottest, windless hours
of the afternoon, well, a seat in a church house
with a high ceiling and a window to the creek—
that's likely the best rest you've found since dawn.

Especially Wednesday nights, pews didn't matter.
You were shoulder-to-shoulder, hip-to-hip,
knees-to-linoleum beside those faithful few
who came to pray, to summon a God they not
only believed in, but who, you believed, cared;
to court the Divine with old familiar words of love.
Our *thees* and *thous* resounded off the walls.
Now I'm no longer quite that kind of faithful.
My theology? I suspect they'd hardly call me
in the fold. But I can think of far worse ways
to spend a summer evening, than kneeling
in the company of thirsty souls who want this:

to press their lips against the fleshy ear of God.

Dairymen at Prayer Meeting

Their foreheads shone where seed caps curled
above their brows, shadowing eyes
that squinted each day down long rows
of soybeans, fodder corn, turning oats.

Their overalls shone too, bright blue,
when, hard-scrubbed, they came to hear
the Word read aloud, in a tongue they grew
to believe the low-toned dialect of God.

At close they knelt to face the pews
and fold swollen hands that stank
of antiseptic wash, tough and pink,
stiff with milking twice each day

forever. I don't recall a moment's doubt
that the Lord heard every syllable,
a Father God who'd surely known
heartaches, troubles enough of his own:

wind, maybe, when wheat was fit to cut,
a girl gone wrong in the noise of town,
deaf to the warnings of Love's hard voice.
Or that one good son, who died so young.

Rain on a Barn South of Tawas

It may be as close as an old man in Michigan
comes to the sound of the sea. Call it thunder
if you want, but it's not thunder, not today.
It's more like the rush of semis on a freeway

somewhere between Bay City and Flint,
the road a son will take when he learns,
sometime around the last taste of a strap,
that the life he was born to is nothing

at all like a life he'd ever bother to live.
There's an anger in it, a tin-edged constancy
that has no rhythm, quite, something more
like white noise that still won't let you sleep.

Think of some man, needing to get a crop in,
but the fields are sop, so he's trying to find
something to fix, something to keep his hands
working, something to weld, something to pound,

something to wrap his calloused palms around
that might do less damage than a lead-rope
knotted and tossed over the limb of a tree.
If you ever decide to lose your years

by working this land, you might think again
about the barn you build, or roofing it with tin.

The Witness

The church-house stank of crumbling cinderblock
and varnish, but their pew glowed like four fresh stumps,
their towheads yellow as the collars on their Goodwill shirts.

With nowhere else to go, the Blanton boys agreed:
they all liked church better than home. And when
the preacher said, *Young folks, to your classes now,*

they laughed and hopped the steps all the way
to Sunday School. They came to such bliss by the grace
and Chevy of their neighbor, a six-cow dairyman, Arden Miller,

who, during testimony time, tried each Lord's Day
to weep back his soul with nose-blown contrition.
He was sure he'd committed, in the candle-heat of youth,

a sin, unpardoned and unpardonable.
This hell—and the hell to come—made him a witness.
Ruth, his wife, had tasted brimstone too, though mostly just

from being near him. Their grief was more than public.
And their care for the souls of the Blanton boys was true,
especially these mornings when they piled down

from Merle Freeman's hired-hand's lean-to house
and jumped in Arden's truck. Six years he hauled them
all to church, dreading they'd go the way he'd gone,

having learned the Good News much too late.
Traveling home, he bought them root beer and coney dogs
and asked, *Boys, do you know you're saved?*

They reckoned they most likely were, and thanked him.
He prayed each morning for their souls, and wept
his way through a second wife, and beat his cows.

God Crazy

Because he didn't ever go to church
Aunt Hazel said Cookie was mad at God.
We'd see him everywhere else, always out
walking somewhere, his shoulders hunched
against the wind, even in the still of the day.

He kept his head down like he'd lost
his watch, and my cousin Kilby swore
the old fart had found more arrowheads
than most anybody who'd ever lived.
But what Kilby knew would rattle in a thimble.

I don't know that he was really looking.
Once Aunt Hazel sent me up to his place
to borrow a gallon of gas for her truck,
not thinking that it was his suppertime.
He asked if I'd eaten, and I couldn't lie.

So he kicked me a chair back, and I sat
while he opened a can. The counter
was clean enough, and his plates were clean
too, thick and dark brown, about the tone
of his hands. He lit the stove and asked,

"You want an egg on your grits?"
and I said, "Yessir," though I'd not
had grits before, and he scooped them on
my plate beside something I know now
was Spam. It was delicious, exotic—

you'd never even notice how the house
smelled of Copenhagen and kerosene.
"There's your Logan County smorgasbord,"
he said. I didn't know where that was
or what he meant, so I just took a slice

of bread from the bag to wipe my plate
and thanked him a lot. He didn't say much
else, but there was a banjo on the bed.
He saw me look at it, and he picked it up
and frailed a tune. That was angel music.

After that day he'd nod when he'd see me
see him walking between the creek and tracks,
hunched over, and I knew he wasn't any
kind of crazy, just thinking of somewhere else,
Logan County maybe, or maybe heaven.

Tilly Read of the Dust Bowl

and she read with a thankful heart.
Newly wed in the Great Depression,
with two girls to raise, one rare Sunday

she sat with a borrowed paper and prayed
for Oklahoma, a place she'd heard
mentioned in songs but would never see.

For an hour, then, with both babies asleep,
she didn't remember her husband's
precarious job in a wrecking yard,

how little flour remained in the bin,
or even how the shame of her shoes
had kept her from church. Instead,

she thought of how green the ash trees
stood along Bokes Creek, how lovely
the lilacs that draped above the privy,

and how, with Frank off hunting turtle,
unless the girls woke, she had a good
half an afternoon to sit at the table

and read her sister-in-law's newspaper,
all that in a room where nothing, nothing
was dusty. *Lord, Lord, those poor folks.*

The Sounds That Feed Us

Stretched beneath the maples
    in the Culver Creek churchyard,
tables spread out like Canaan
    for dinner on the grounds.
What a hot and holy buzz:
    women chattering the covers off
their most requested dishes,
    a pickup quartet practicing
in the church house, their chords
    drifting through the windows,
old folks chewing, spitting, fanning,
    children squabbling as they scramble
around their mothers' weary feet,
    young folks stealing hats
and shrieking through a game
    of keep-away which looks
like courting, and beneath it all,
    the low hum of bumble bees
gathering around the privies,
    strafing the casseroles
and sweet tea, the relish, the babies,
    the honeysuckle. In my memory
it's all music. And the finest voice is
    Miss Liza Langrall's coconut cake.

Resurrection

My neighbor—she's just turned five—asked me,
"What's *your* favorite Bible story, Bill?" So
I fudged it. "I love all kinds of stories," I tell her.

I could hardly say *this*: Listen, kid, my church
was a holiness church, our God wore Redwings,
and he'd shake you by the scruff of your neck

if you didn't mind your *p*'s and *q*'s. Got it?
I grew up with a healthy fear of tent stakes,
and I can't swim in whale-infested waters.

I have a penchant toward fig leaf briefs.
And, I might add, for me the lake of fire
and brimstone is as real as your bowl of blueberries.

I also have the ability to swallow, digest,
even memorize telephone-book-sized lists
of nonsense, like God loves Jews the best—

and all holiness people, at least the faithful
at Culver Creek Holiness, are really Jews.
Don't even ask how we explain that one,

or how I discovered my call to take God's love
to dark, naked people in tropical climates
just as I was entering puberty. Add to that

a willingness to personify and discern
the sacred nature of whirlwinds, earthquakes,
thunderstorms, already-full parking lots,

pork lasagna, and coconut cake, which leads
to a deep sense of my own complete perfection,
held in tension with my contempt for and terror

of my deep perversity. With all that going on,
there wasn't much room for a favorite Bible story.
But listen, little one, yours was a good question:
I have always loved spring, and every empty tomb.

Part Four

One Wheel in the Furrow

Spring Plowing

God knows it's slow work, especially
when March streams like a broken faucet,
or gluttonous snows fall through February.

You batter the gates till you can't stand it,
then you try. . . . Next thing you know,
you're axle deep in a dead furrow

or your rig sinks like a big green boat
above some broken drain tile. You can bury
yourself in any square foot that lays low.

But you can only gnaw the stall door so long.
My father would suffer the weather
for days or weeks at a time, hovering

inside the kitchen like a dry gray cloud,
having changed the oil in every engine
and greased every conceivable part,

waiting, waiting, *good God*, for better weather.
And that, Gentle Reader, is why I left
the farm.

But there were other days, magazine-cover
tractor-ad days, when the ground turned itself
over, the way a woman peels away her robe,

anxious to be loved. The very wind
smelled of apple flowers and diesel smoke,
and you believed you were born for a reason.

The Best Novembers

When fall was dry and the grain turned
early, my father sometimes kept a child
or two at home to start the plowing.

Working ground—what a relief it was
from the other jobs a boy must do:
just keep one wheel in the furrow,

listen to the engine's strain, watch
the moldboards for stalk jams and rocks,
and that's all. Perched far and away

from the curses of school and the clouds
of the house, I could rest for ten, maybe
twelve hours, riding the calm vibration

of the diesel, sipping warmth from a stone
mug, watching the golden stubble turn
beneath deep ridges the color of coffee

with real cream. It made the world seem
safe and small to feel my right front wheel
steer itself down a clean, dark furrow, to know
just where I was going, exactly where I'd been.

The Sheep Farmer

You tromped our morning kitchen in gum boots,
stirred a little coffee in your sugar,
gave me sips, asked me things, and listened.
The rest I know about you came too late

to dim or lessen what you were to me:
a daily blessing, a saint with wizard hair
that strayed across your face, a magical scent
(it may've been the sheep), and strange scars

lifting like runes on your wrists and arms.
Neighbors who heard you sing above the roar
of an engine (with your perfect knowledge
of Methodist hymns) would never have guessed

your struggles in the shadows, your *dark spells*.
I didn't know then—why would I?—how hard
you worked to live, how often you tried to die,
that the lines that tied you to life were so thin.

I only knew you whole. And I hear your voice
still now, the nodding rhythm of your prayer,
your tones that wrapped each word in taut felt,
your hands a steepled church above your plate,

an offering, maybe, to the old god you fought.
I don't know. What good is memory, if it's not
forgiving? Let me be the one to say your grace:
We thank thee, Lord, for life and the joy of living.

Whatever Was Ripe

The poor Uncle knew had no Hollywood stars
to dance through the satellite skies,
to raise *just a few pennies per day*
for whatever that stuff is, white corn mush maybe,

that Barbie and Ken, popular prime time hosts
of *True Death Stories*, dump in each kid's cup.
The poor he knew were not gray strangers
in ectoplastic lines waiting for soup

from Cincinnati nurses on furlough,
a group of concerned teachers from Dayton,
or the Baptist Youth on Love-Serve Projects,
learning to embrace the pain of others.

Except for Uncle, these poor were alone:
displaced Appalachians mostly,
once removed from coal mines or their own farms.
In time, they learned to listen for hunger

in their children's breath, an unfamiliar sound
that came to them slowly, the knowing of it,
like the sharp twisting in their own guts
that, slowly too, they'd come to recognize.

If the Lord thy God were paying
a boohoo bunch of attention,
Kilby, Uncle's sister Wanda's boy said,
you wouldn't have to pump this water—

it'd be rainin' grits and cigarettes
in Fulton County. But Uncle didn't hear
so well at times, and he went on out
to squawk the handle all evening,

tending six acres of corn and green beans,
red beans and tomatoes, and finally
the two rows of mild peppers he nursed
through drought like small, full-bellied children—

only to give it all away, all he grew,
to whoever got word that it was ready.
Some days the ditches were lined
with rusty vans and pickups,

fruits of the state's high employment rate
our recovering economy, of which we
Ohioans have every right to be proud,
who, on their way home from the split shift

at Dixie Mart, two dollars an hour,
filled sacks and buckets with whatever
Uncle said was ripe. Or near enough to ripe.
Shoot me for a fool, Kilby stomped,

if you weren't my mama's brother,
I'd say you're one crazy briarhopper.
But Uncle never stopped humming.
He just sank deeper into the earth,

gently now on his new plastic hip,
to pull a thistle or a buttonweed maybe,
his voice turning rich and low, working
his music down among the rows of melons.

The Funerals of Poor People

Even their cars can tell you this:
poor people have to die too.
They wait, parked in the lot outside
the funeral home, dressed in rust
and age, and sometimes tasteless
stickers and window ornaments.
But the little flags the undertaker uses
fit their antennae just the same.
Leaving the building, the mourners'

clothes whisper about being poor.
If the women wear navy, sometimes
the pumps are not quite the right tone
for the dresses . . . some even fake it
with black. The men seem to wear
dark suits but if you look closely,
sometimes the jackets and slacks
don't quite match. All this is true
but then, who should really care

with so much other sorrow? The poor
have less to start with, so might
the loss of some good body be
a deeper red in the debit column?
It's not easy to lose a friend, and
it's not easy to die or be poor. Imagine
wondering if your old car will start
again at the cemetery, or if you'll have
to walk back to town in borrowed shoes.

Communion at Union City Mission

At the Union City Mission, bent men file by
the altar and cross the stage. They shake
our hands, then take a short-cut to the kitchen
where macaroni and cheese, day-old cake,
and weak coffee repay their patience.
A few smell of wine and most of sweat,
and they know it: you can't get all-over clean
without a shower or a real bathroom.
Only the most grimly sodden don't care.

One gray drunk lets others pass around him.
He's trying to wrench a pink pocket comb,
its teeth as broken as his own, through his hair.
He's distracted, like an old woman who checks
her nose on the church steps, to get it just right.
He's waiting to talk. Maybe he liked the banjo.
Maybe he used to be salesman-of-the-month.
Maybe he's glad our music saved his scuffed soul
from one more sermon about some other hell.

For Charlie, in Lucasville Prison

Is there a final kick that makes a killer?
Had his father beat him one less time,
would he be a math instructor now?

Is there a cuff that makes the mind click
from salesman to hit-man, from machinist
to murderer, from saint to politician?

And is there some great work of grace that turns
the grinding stone around, that makes the meal
turn back to corn, happy and whole?

I knew a man who used his brain and back
to make a hillbilly fortune the only way
open to him. He was deeply loved

and deeply hated, sometimes by the same
folks, sometimes on the same day. Did
something go right or something go wrong?

Getting where he got took muscle. By the end
he carried a knife in his pocket, a Ruger pistol
under his truck seat, and a magazine of cash

chained to his hip. Maybe carrying such things
is a burden, and the weight just wore him out.
That's what his lawyer said, and I believe him.
And who among us knows what else he had to haul?

Felon

My finger swelled to twice its size.
It was warm to touch and red and black,
and even the best salve Mom had bought
from the traveling agent wouldn't draw.

So she talked with my father, who shook
his head but brought her up the iron
skillet from my granny's box of special
things they kept beneath the steps.

She put in flour and pepper and milk
and dust from a tobacco tin,
and she stirred it all in that little black
skillet, whispering all the time.

When it started to make, all brown and thick,
she scraped the rim with a piece of lathe
and spooned it on my finger, smoking hot.
I cried, hard. She made tears too,

but didn't stop a minute, just kept on
with her whispers. At last she wrapped
my hand, heavy but loose, in strips
from a clean white sheet, and set me

down, whimpering, by the woodstove.
I couldn't sleep, so Granny stayed with me.
In the darkness I could hear her whisper,
There's times this is how we have to do.

The next morning my finger burned some,
but the swelling and pus were gone,
gone and didn't come back, though sometimes
when the world gets dark, I feel it there still.

Why the Laundromat Lady Is So Fat

In Glenna's eyes,
the remains of gray
skies, 1938.

And a rented house
in Pinesburg, Ohio,
on a sad morning

when ice hung on
every sad branch
of the weeping willow,

and a meanish wind
crackled them
like the bone staves

of her first girdle
or starched skirt,
when her mother

had gone to cook
breakfast at a roadhouse
where chattery men

who had jobs
for the county ate.
And her father

had no work
and was mean
as an old skunk

even when he did.
He was a hurtful man,
and big, too big,

as she later told it,
and she laughed
and ate and ate.

She could cook
just like her mom,
and sometimes

that was enough
to make him lay off.
Not like later,

when the money
and coal were gone
and there was nothing,

nothing but anger
and too many months of winter.

Thanksgiving

Because my father, whose grease-caked hands
were never without reason, wrench, or dream,
would, even on evenings when he needed me,
sometimes let me grab my fishing gear and go;

and our land, which lay in fence-rowed tracts
as far as my small eyes or feet could run,
never called me stranger or turned its back,
but let me follow its corn-rowed furrows;

and the river, whose banks were my refuge
and salvation, would raise high and muddy
shoulders, then drop down clear and dark
and razor thin for my contemplations;

this ease I feel when I'm driving and spot
a line of willow and ash winding through
a worked field, about sundown, can sweeten
even these bitter lips toward thanksgiving.

Dust of the Gods

Hints of something like heaven happen, sometimes
with cures for cancer or drought, but at other times
when a boy is harrowing ahead of the corn planter,
his twelfth hour on a tractor seat, and he breathes
the trail of diesel fumes, grows nauseous with the stench
and the heat of spring and the brilliance of the May sun,
then sees, around the fissures a migraine has cut
through his vision, a little whirlwind moving, hovering
over the acres, spinning toward him, knowing him,
calling his name like some North African dervish
he would not read about for years to come,
but as he drives he waits for Elisha's electric voice,
and although he doesn't hear it, he learns the way light
can shine through pain, and he learns to keep listening.

Part Five

The Garden Again

Sermon for a Monday

Therefore the Lord God sent him forth from the garden of Eden, to till the ground from whence he was taken. (Genesis 3:23)

A body grows old, holding all that sadness,
    bearing it like a tumor.
The back bends crooked, offering all that care,
    hunching in accustomed pain.
The trunk twists, spreading heavy branches so wide,
    and the earth beneath turns dry.

The feet and knees that drag the body to work
    race up a hill that needn't be a hill.
The truck chokes and shudders down a gear,
    grieved that it cannot go fast.
A tornado is coming! Hide in the cellar!
    We can live in the musty dark.

Wisdom, being small, demands that we use it,
    those little wisps we've managed to gather.
Two great teachings of our good old brother:
    It is finished. Remember the lilies.
So let's be sad together, weep in the floods
    of all that childhood heartbreak.

Maybe we should rub our faces in pasture grass,
    even though the cows have grazed here.
Maybe we should roll in heaps of crimson leaves,
    even though we know the snow comes next.
This world is a sad and hostile place. It is also Paradise.

The Art of Augury

Every prophet has a favorite technique.
Take cephalomancy: though rare today,
it tells the future by boiling the heads
of donkeys. It's been proven accurate

in foretelling the sudden appearance
of large, dead mammals on the patio.
Or felidomancy: observation
of feline behavior. Time and again

it's foretold the arrival and payment
of carpet cleaners. Or anthropomancy:
that's the study of sacrificed humans—
the most common, yet the most useful, too—

and it's not hard. My amateur attempts
have successfully prophesied divorce,
bankruptcy, and despair, all with frantic
accuracy. First, watch how people slave

to pay bills, raise kids, and make love stay.
Second, notice how they don't. I'll confess,
any of the methods work. The wonder
is that we've ever been surprised at all.

The Way We Live with Sorrow

It's a blessing, the way time settles in:
the cartilage between bony sorrows.
Friends die, but they don't all die at once.

The first gives way to cancer, slowly,
then weeks go by, years if you're young
or lucky. Then a second passes on,

multiple sclerosis or maybe AIDS.
Maybe heart failure. The pain you feel
for each loss is great, but time passes

and quilts a soft cushion. Eventually
you grow a muscle to suffer with.
Hours and years let you do that. Imagine

if your children all left home at once—
that would be unbearable. Devastating.
But one goes to college, one marries,

the last buys a zither and a microbus
and sings on the streets. It's only time,
the natural progression, that saves you

from the density of black that would seal
us all in some pneumatic tube of dread.
I explained this to a student whose true

love thought he'd become a baseball star.
He didn't. Be thankful for the hours,
I tell him, the hours between sorrows:

first a lover goes—you think she's just
gone for the day. That's healthy space.
You live with that, then a week passes,

a month, you cry when you see her
toothbrush, her last bag of granola, but
sadness is softened by all the time since.

You've taken up cribbage or violin,
and you're deeply engaged. Distracted.
Then she calls to say she's not coming back,

and by then it's not so bad. Like amputation.
You hope to keep all your limbs, but one goes,
and you soon learn to limp along, or even
to make music in a sparse, one-handed way.

Online Registration for Fall Term

I feel like some mess of a freshman,
she says, *but it's all so tangled up
and I can't make it work. It won't!*

Her fingers twist knots in her hair,
and a strand of snot drifts from her lip
to her shoulder. I turn off the screen

and, surreptitiously, draw out
four sheets of paper, softly lined,
lay them down like the four corners

of the world, and divide each one
into two semesters, true yellow weeks
and fountain-blue days. We fill in

work-study, general requirements,
major prerequisites, madrigal choir.
She blows her nose a little less often.

Every kitchen has a junk drawer,
I tell her, *and sometimes you just
dump it out and sort it.* She smiles,

*But I feel like that ball of string
my crazy grandma crammed in there
with her can lids and paper clips*

*and the loose screws from things
she can't fix.* Bless you, daughter.
If it were not unethical, illegal,

and so utterly out of my character,
I believe I could embrace you
now, like the very mother of God.

From Where I Stood

On the trail to South Falls you ran ahead.
I watched your caps, red, brown, and green,
like furtive birds hungry for spring,
disappear around the first switchback.
So you were lost forever until I leaned
against a railing to take a picture—
then that was you, dancing in and out behind
the torrent. You may have heard my heart.

The ledge looked so narrow, the falls so high,
the railing so rickety, the rock so slick. . . .
You fell together a thousand times
like wooden blocks bouncing down steps
before I reached you, before I knew
that what seemed so perilous from above
was tame below, the ledge thirty feet wide,
the drop beneath the water's course, gradual.

No matter. I watch you all yet as you slide
toward your destruction—that's my despair,
when each night hasn't had enough
troubles of its own, and I need some
rancid dream to break my hope of sleep,
to drive me to the bathroom and flip on a light,
to remind me of how the heart sometimes flies,
just when I think I've forgotten how to love.

Family Band at Union Gospel Mission

How long can they stay here? my son asks as we leave
through the double-locked doors. We've played

our music here before, so he's known the brogan stomp,
the stench of old sweat, the wine-damp tears,

but never in winter, never in such packed and steamy rows
of hangdog faces and half-stoned babble, dirty as snow,

a few with children in hand. I've asked myself that
from another angle: *How long can they stand it—*

and stay here? When is the limit reached, when do things
get better or get over? I've talked to some who choose

the privacy of an overpass or the safety of a sewer grate
over a set of Christian sheets. But cold is cold,

and tonight the born-again beds are full. With luck,
our aging van will limp on home and make our piece

of debt and plywood seem more or less like heaven,
which is exactly what we've been singing about.

And which we'll sing about again next month,
next year, and for as long as Chaplain Gary says,

You and your kids are all the fellas' favorites.
For some, maybe it's half an hour of paradise. For others,

aching for beans and macaroni, for warm, brackish coffee
and someone's unclaimed day-old wedding cake

just one room over, the only real question may be
How long, O Lord, how long are these folks gonna play?

The Fuse Box

This chest feels like it's locked.
But under my ribs, where my heart
should be, I believe you'll find

an old fuse box, the steel-gray type
with a press-to-latch door and red flecks
of rust erupting through the paint

and holes for a padlock no one uses.
It's the kind of box you only see
these days in clapboard houses

on farmsteads that haven't been
lived in for years or bulldozed yet,
with hip-roofed sleeping garrets

and mud-rooms slumping toward
the barn, and maybe three real rooms—
as much a house as I could ever live in.

And in the box are slots for three green
and yellow fuses, but they're gone,
and some poor, dumb briarhopper

(that'd be me) has pressed pennies in,
so that no matter what you run or where
you plug it in, the circuits just won't

blow, it all just keeps on cycling.
Then even when the house burns down,
as such houses do, forever and ever

there'll be a tangle of copper wire
in the ashes, telling almost everything
as well as I ever could about what
it's meant for me to be your father.

The Least We Owe

For weeks she'd said, "Come see me skate,"
and I slipped other duties in the way,
reports and proposals, meetings without end.

It was easy to let months pass. Her sport was
not a competition or performance: it was just
the cut-rate Friday morning open skate

at the dingy local rink where she practiced laps.
The season nearly passed before a mix of guilt
and laziness drove me to *Great Skates Alive*,

where I bought an Americano, sat in the bleachers
with Faulkner in hand, and scanned the ice
for stocky pre-teen forms. Hers wasn't there—

but there, first arched in flight on the rink's far side,
then pumping hard, gliding and sailing, swooping
like an angry gull, in and out, circling the other skaters,

she sailed past me, and saw me, I'm pretty sure.
But she had other tricks to try, with names I know
only during Olympic years. I hope with all her moves

she's learned forgiveness, too, for her blind father.
Please see me like I really am inside, she meant to say.
Trapped in a world of slim, athletic siblings and friends,

she wanted me to know her in this sacred space,
to follow her angelic arabesque, to watch her body
as she sometimes loves and feels it, to see her

as she sees her deepest self, if only for an hour
on Friday mornings. Maybe that's the least we owe
our children. Maybe that's the least we owe ourselves.

Leaf Fall

I've walked these trails more than one afternoon
and watched as some tree, like its kin in every detail,
surrenders its leaves in one thick falling, a pouring,

less a storm than a blessing. An hour later, maybe two,
it stands there bare, scribbling the sky in tangled gray,
with its sisters still wrapped bright in a palette of autumn.

A botanist is one of the things I'm not, but I've searched
for a reason—more or less water or shade or wind?—
and found none, no cause to claim but the fullness of time.

Today is the time at our house. The maple we planted
the year we moved in is *right now* letting go. So I turn
my chair around to face the window, even as I listen

to you, packing boxes in your room, almost ready.
The single leaves, it seems to me, fall ever so slowly,
but the suddenness with which they're all gone, just
gone, leaves me old and dull, maybe a little stunned.

When the Children Go Away

In their absence the soul moves out of the house
and builds a lean-to behind the kitchen.
It sleeps on a cot, drinks instant Folgers, smokes,
and never reads a book beyond the first chapter.

In their absence the soul goes back to bed.
It only rises to phone in sick. It won't
listen to the worries of befuddled new hires.
It turns its aching neck against the pillow.

To say *The life has gone out of the wine*
would demand more reason than remains.
No half-romantic drunk, no kindly buzz,
just the heavy head, just the faint smell of gas

and grits boiling over a dull circle of flame.
Maybe tomorrow it will shake its own hand
for choosing not to die. Tomorrow it may
leave its woolen blankets and wash its face.

Pilgrims' Road

On days when the tunnel around my heart
was dangerously dark, when my soul felt
like a truck had slipped from the jacks
and fallen hard on my chest, I would stick

a note to my door, sneak out the back
of University Hall, and head south.
In an hour I would be walking the aisles
of Walmart, adrift in the talking-songs

of those homefolk angels in polyester,
floating in the warm flood of their vowels.
In the pale blue labyrinth of cheap plastic
and cellophane cupcakes, I could rest.

Now that I'm old, the truck lightens up
most days, and right now I'm feeling no pain.
I'm reading a postcard from my daughter,
a pilgrim on *El Camino de Santiago.*

Today she's traveling toward Santo Domingo,
to a quirky medieval cathedral where
alongside the icons, a sacred pair of chickens,
alive and clucking, bless the old and holy space.

I pray she finds her way, that in the ache
of her back, in the blisters she breaks today,
she'll find her reasons for walking, or at least
the twisted shapes of light our Lord can take.

I don't know if she will. And I don't know if
she'll know if she does. But this I do believe:
if the polyester angels who sustained my soul
had built a cathedral, it would've had chickens.

The Garden Again

In the sweat of thy face shalt thou eat bread, till thou return unto the ground.
(Genesis 3:19)

It begins as sod, a summer's worth of stubble,
a winter's worth of blackberry, grass, and vines,
of whatever too was left to rot last November
when the woman said *enough* and gave it up.

This little piece of the planet has returned
to something like its own nature—you can call it
a scab, but a healthy, healing scab on the earth's
fleshy cheek. Now it's time to pick at it again.

Beneath the french-kissing tongue of the spade,
the sod becomes a menage of clods, a jumble
of roots and stems and leaves chopped for soup,
black melons, old tomatoes decayed in the clay.

Then a little April rain, then a little May sun,
then the hoe, and the clods break in a passion
of metal and sweat. Another rain, more sun,
and the flesh roils with a sweet brown promise.

Planting day: the lines are stretched, the rake takes
its turn, the chunks roll and crumble beneath
the back and forth of the tines, and hours turn
the patch to soft pebbles maybe, or coffee grounds.

So it's nothing like nature now, but it's good,
and the seeds go in, and more rain, and weeks
happen, and something like the way love works
breaks out beneath the sagging strands of twine.

Acknowledgments

I thank the editors of the following publications in which some of these poems first appeared, often in slightly different form:

Apalachee Review: "Dust of the Gods"
Blue Collar Review: "Rain on a Barn South of Tawas"
Briar Cliff Review: "When the Children Go Away"
Borderlands: The Texas Poetry Review: "Pictures of Katie," "Noah's Children"
Chaffin Journal: "Thanksgiving"
The Christian Century: "Reach Hither Thy Finger"
Coe Review: "The Prophet Amos Adds a Postscript"
Compass Rose: "The Least We Owe"
Connecticut River Review: "The Art of Augury," "The Vigil on the Corner"
The Distillery: "Best Novembers"
Exit 13: "Leaf Fall"
Friends Journal: "The Hardness of the Pews," "The Sounds That Feed Us"
Literature and Belief: "Ways to Die," "Legion's Farewell to the Gerasenes,"
     "Ananias's Confession"
Midwest Quarterly: "The Fuse Box"
Pearl: "Felon"
Pennsylvania English: "Small College, Small Town," "The Price of Salvation"
Plainsongs: "Communion at Union City Mission"
POEM: "Tilly Read of the Dust Bowl," "The Sheep Farmer"
South Dakota Review: "The Witness," "God Crazy"
Southern Poetry Review: "Touching Abishag," "Why the Laundromat Lady
     Is So Fat"
Sou'wester: "Whatever Was Ripe"
The Sow's Ear Poetry Review: "For Charlie, in Lucasville"
Sundog: The Southeast Review: "The Last Pasture"

Acknowledgments

Sycamore Review: "The Funerals of Poor People"

West Branch: "Steers In Winter," "Age and Belief," "Spring Plowing"

Willow Review: "A Blessing," "Big Bang," "Online Registration for Fall Term," "From Where I Stood," "Family Band at Union Gospel Mission"

Windhover: "Diet of Worms"

Writer's Forum: "Adam Walks"

Many of the poems in Part One appeared in *Searching for a White Crow* (Pudding House Press). "Whatever Was Ripe" appeared in the chapbook *Whatever Was Ripe* (Bright Hill Press).

COLLECTIONS IN THIS SERIES INCLUDE: